Applied Sociology

Sociological Understanding and its Application

Jerry S. Maneker

University Press of America, Inc.
Lanham • New York • London

University Press of America,® Inc.
4720 Boston Way
Lanham, Maryland 20706

3 Henrietta Street
London, WC2E 8LU England

Library of Congress Cataloging-in-Publication Data
Maneker, Jerry S.
Applied sociology : sociological understanding
and its application / Jerry S. Maneker.
p.   cm.
Includes bibliographical references.
1. Sociology.   2. Social problems.   I.   Title.
HM51 . M239   1994
301--dc20   94-24360 CIP

ISBN 0-8191-9777-7 (pbk.: alk paper)

⊖™The paper used in this publication meets the minimum
requirements of American National Standard for Information
Sciences—Permanence of Paper for Printed Library Materials,
ANSI Z39.48–1984.

Dedicated to Eileen, the light of my life

Contents

Introduction

Toward an Applied Sociology

It has long been recognized by behavioral and social scientists that one's neurobiology effects one's social functioning. Through animal studies and clinical experience it seems that childhood traumas, and perhaps adult traumas, can become encoded and permanently effect one's neurobiology. Through what is called "Kindling," increasingly slighter traumas may escalate and, hence, one's neurobiology may well distort and disfigure one's temperament and personality. (For an excellent discussion of this and related topics see Listening to Prozac, by Peter D. Kramer, Viking Press, 1993.) Perhaps this ensuing biological disfigurement may be genetically passed on to subsequent generations.

Therefore, as scientists and professionals, it behooves us to not merely study social institutions, but also prescribe remedies so that these institutions may become more amenable to the highest levels of human needs and aspirations which, in my opinion, we were enjoined to do by C. Wright Mills in his book The Sociological Imagination. What Sociologists do is akin to the following scenario: a patient is told by his physician that he has appendicitis. The doctor then bids him a good day. Who would go to such a physician? Why would the medical profession be held in high esteem if all it could do is diagnose ailments, with no hope of relief to the patient? Sociologists are currently in that very position whereby we barely diagnose, let alone suggest, courses of treatment to our institutional "patients." This factor may be key in our relatively precarious status within academe and in the society at large. After all, how often do we see the media represented at our regional and national meetings?

It seems to me that we must both diagnose and suggest remedies to the institutions we study to foster individual life affirmation, wholeness, creativity, comfort, security, and acceptance of people's uniqueness. After all, if undesirable personality traits can be "Kindled," so can desirable ones. Psychopharmacology, particularly the drug Prozac, presumably given its effect on the neurotransmitter Serotonin, can make a shy person more assertive; an anxious person more tranquil; a thoughtful person more decisive; an anhedonic more pleasure-seeking; a melancholy person more vivacious. As Kramer points out, these personality traits are highly valued in our contemporary, competitive, get it while you can society. Psychopharmacology certainly has its place and in many ways has been of enormous benefit to many suffering people. However, as Sociologists we must work from the other end of the matrix.

Do we want a society of assertive, competitive, conforming pleasure-seekers with "tolerable" amounts of sociopathy? Do we want to risk losing the art, poetry, literature, and even science that springs from the struggling mind of the melancholic, the seeker after truth and self, the stranger in a strange land? Should Sociology be the social scientific equivalent of a mind candy that closes its eyes to the disfigured institutions and their resultant personalities in our midst?

What I am suggesting is that we be both a "Science" (studying social institutions) and a "Profession" (suggesting remedies to these institutions) that meet the aforementioned highest aspirations and needs of people in this and future generations. Such phenomena as violence, greed, crime, and sociopathy are symptoms crying out for relief. In sum, I am suggesting that many life-draining and disfiguring institutions, and the people who run amok amidst their chaos, are, in part, the consequence of our lethargy as a discipline and as a profession.

The chapters which follow represent attempts to apply or harness Sociology and its unique perspective to various human and organizational problems that currently beset us. It is my firm belief that by applying the "Science" of Sociology to these problems, we may create a "Profession" every bit as necessary to our welfare as is the profession of medicine. If Sociology is not applied toward enhancing the quality of life for people, its rationale for existence is at the very least highly questionable.

Chapter One

On Applied Sociology: The Institutionalization of Marginality*

"Applied Sociology" may be seen to come to analytical and empirical terms with Mills; dictum that we must view history and biography as an interrelated whole. Only when people become conscious of their community of interests, and develop a "sociological imagination," can they be inclined to relieve themselves of guilt attendant upon accepting the burden for their alienation or anomie (where one's expectations exceed what society delivers) and place that burden where it frequently belongs: on the social structure. There are two interrelated approaches one takes in the area of applied sociology, therefore. The first approach, as witnessed in this chapter, is to awaken consciousness--or dissipate "false consciousness."[2] This can be done by sociologically analyzing common human and social problems and by making people aware of these analyses so that a community of recognized interests may be awakened. The second approach occurs in the "field" where the sociologist, on the basis of the first approach, mobilizes motivation to redress grievances and help organize strategy to satisfy that motivation.

By "marginality" we mean a state whereby the person is insufficiently integrated into the dominant culture or, perhaps, even into his subculture. He is "the stranger," "the outsider," "the man without a country," "the outcast," "the misfit." This person may be marginal in fact or in his perception, which becomes reality for him. Marginality seems to be one of the most pervasive and yet little known institutions in our society. Until we analytically and empirically come to grips with this realization, applied sociology and the attendant mobilized motivations remain ideals rather than a viable alternatives to apathy and alienation.

To postulate that marginality is institutionalized in our society implies three concurrent phenomena. The first phenomenon relates to the definition of "institution." An institution is an established way of doing things.[3] It is usually functional for the society of which it is a more or less viable locus. The pervasiveness of marginality, to be discussed below, seems to be a well established principle to infer that it is similarly established in our society. The second phenomenon relates to the definition of "marginality."[4] This term may be seen to be the structural correlate of the social psychological conditions of alienation and anomie. Here, the individual is in a social structural twilight zone within a more or less acceptable institutional framework. He is on the outside looking in, and frequently sees distorted images, projected by his perceptions of the reality. The third phenomenon suggests the functional utility of marginality (in line with the first phenomenon). We each have a vested interest (to be discussed below) in keeping ourselves and each other marginal. It seems functional for society as a whole (not a reification, but with a contemporary Durkheimian[5] perspective) that many individuals and subgroups become and remain marginal to other individuals, subgroups, and dominant organizations and other institutions in society.

The preceding discussion sets the stage to analyze who is marginal and why. Here we are not interested in types of marginal people, but in the pervasiveness of marginality, its apparent genesis, and its raison d'etre (or its functions).

Who is marginal? Children,[6] adolescents,[7] women,[8] minority groups, "deviants,"[9] people on welfare, the poor,[10] and the aged.[11] Most people, either at some time in their lives or throughout all their lives, are marginal. But marginal to what? They seem to be marginal to the social patterns that are expected on the basis of their socialization. That is to say, most people are marginal to a reference group they have been socialized to regard highly. For children and adolescents it is adulthood. For ethnic groups it is each other as well as their relationships to the dominant group. For the poor, it is the middle class. For "deviants" it is acceptance, or benign neglect by "straights." For the aged, it is acceptance by the young and middle-aged.[12] In these and in many other cases, people are marginal to a more or less highly valued reference group. One may argue that if one is an integrated member of a subculture, such as that of drug addicts, there is not any outside reference group that he regards highly. This may be true were the subculture contained in a vacuum. However, the potential power of the outgroup to harass and punish the members of this subculture of definition forces members of that subculture to act with no little regard to that outgroup--or, here, reference group, given their behavior in psychological and social reference to that "dominant group." Cohen[13] lends credence to this assumption in his study of delinquency. His view is that juvenile delinquency is a form of natural adaptation to the working class environment. The working class youth is exposed to middle class values which he cannot attain because of social structural constraints. He resolves his dilemma by contriving with others who share in his plight to adjust. They do this by inverting middle class values and denigrating them. Thus arises the delinquent subculture. Here, we are interested in its suggestive implications for social structural contingencies fostering marginality. The working class youth ostensibly has a reference group, the middle class. Yet, he is barred from effective participation with members of that class. Hence, his marginality. To deal with that marginality more or less effectively, he transforms that reference group into an outgroup which both facilitates the formation of an ingroup and allows him some vehicle for retribution on members of the middle class and their values.

Of course, this does not mean that all people who act in reference to other people are marginal. It does mean that when people use certain others to develop an identity of self, and act in regard to those others, be they in proximity to them or not, they view that identification group as a reference group. If they want to make that reference group a membership group and have not as yet been able to do so, they may be viewed as marginal with reference to that group. Although marginality may, and frequently does, occur in reference to one's membership group, we are only interested here in the type of marginality broadly conceived as the social structural correlate of alienation (being estranged from existing norms) and anomie (the absence of norms).

Viewed in this way, we may ask why are so many people marginal? There appears to be two major reasons why so many people are marginal. It will be the discussion of these two reasons that may shed light on one's community of interests with others that may help awaken consciousness of the role of the social structure in the genesis of the functionally useful control mechanisms of marginality. The two reasons deal with the following two concepts: "identity" and "frontiers."

Identity is that which gives one a sense of self. It is dependent upon the way we are socialized and who does the socializing.[14] The former element denotes the "content" of the socialization; the latter element denotes the "form" of the socialization. McLuhan's premise that the form of communication effects the individual far more than does its content[15] leads us to emphasize the latter element in our discussion of identity. Who does the socializing? In other words, given that the content of socialization acts as a control mechanism internalized by the individual (psychoanalysts call it a "superego"), what role does the form of the socialization--that is, who does the socializing and under what conditions-- have in identity development? We should also emphasize that socialization does not stop at any particular age, but goes on throughout one's life. Indeed, we feel that "adult socialization" may even be of greater importance in identity development than is socialization that occurs in one's childhood. Since socialization is learning gotten via communication, and since the form of communication does not necessarily have to take second place to its content, it seems fruitful to examine the role of "form" in identity development.

For our purposes, there seem to be two major kinds of identity: "primary identity" and "secondary identity." These terms denote from what groups (and,

hence, relationships) one derives his concept of self. We are mobile people.[16]
Given the requirements of the nuclear family and job, occupational and
geographical mobility are unbiquitous phenomena in our society.[17] Such
conditions of life seem to require relationships that are secondary rather than
primary in nature. A primary relationship usually occurs in a primary group
characterized by intimate face to face interaction.[18] This type of relationship is
characterized by diffuseness, affectivity and particularism.[19] The relationship is
diffuse in that one responds to another as an integrated whole; a whole human
being. In this relationship one is interested in the other person as a total human
being. The relationship is affective in that one responds to another with feeling,
not solely with intellect. There is emotional investment here, where the
individual deeply cares what happens to the other human being. Involved here is
some "transference" and "identification" where the individual is happy or sad,
proud or mortified on the basis of the actions of the other in the primary
relationship. The relationship is particular in that expectations of the other's
behavior are held up to standards predicated upon emotional involvement with
the other human being in the relationship. In short, we usually have different
standards for our loved ones than we do for the local shop keeper.

A secondary relationship is characterized by specificity, affective neutrality,
and universalism.[20] It usually occurs in a secondary group which is usually
large and has a formal structure. The office, the schoolroom, et cetera are apt
examples. The relationship is specific in that one responds to the other as a
segment--for example, as an economic person. The major interest one
presumably has in his/her employee is that of a worker. He usually does not
care how happy or fulfilled the other is, unless it has bearing on his performance
at work. He does not view the other as a whole person. The relationship is
affectively neutral in that the person usually does not invest his emotions in the
being of the other. The relationship is universalistic in that the individual
applies standards of expectations to the other that in no way takes the other's
unique characteristics, such as they may be, into account.

Secondary relationships are not only unbiquitous in our society, but seem to
be increasingly playing the role of foremost socializing agent. From the time
one enters school, he is involved in secondary relationships with significant
others (friends who when in class become other schoolmates who usually
approve and disapprove behavior). These significant others are teachers and
peers. There orientation toward the person are by and large affectively neutral,
specific, and universalistic. The individual not only becomes a manipulable
object, but increasingly comes to view himself in that light with seemingly
little if any cognitive dissonance (holding two inconsistent beliefs).[21] He
comes to learn, if he is to gain acceptance, he must please others--all sorts of
others. This feeling is reinforced throughout secondary school and college. The
college student quickly learns that the only sure way of doing well in a course is
to memorize the instructors' notes and regurgitate them at exam time. The
material need not be relevant, and frequently is not relevant; it need not be

stimulating; it need not expand the horizons of the student. It need fill only one criterion: it must be memorizable. Many students appear to become anxious when asked to express their ideas. Some seem devoid of ideas in a broad subject area, and many more appear to fear the ridicule of their fellow students should they appear too dense or too profound.

School then may be seen to become a training ground for the stereotyped organization man. The person who works hard and forgets what for. The person reluctant to question anything. Higher education has as its ideal goal to turn out scholars. We may define a scholar as one who questions everything-- "everything." Not only do college graduates seem reluctant to question anything, but have a vested interest in not questioning anything--particularly if it pertains to the social structure. They have a vested interest in being apathetic. Their apathy may be seen to spring from their marginality, and reinforces that marginality, by encouraging blindness to effective alternatives to cope with the contingencies of their existence. We seem to have a vested interest in keeping ourselves apathetic, and hence marginal. By remaining marginal, we seem better able to set up boundaries that reaffirm our identities.

We may be seen to have a vested interest in keeping ourselves marginal because of the type of identity we have developed. We need boundaries based on apathy to reaffirm an existence and not a life. Moreover, we have a vested interest in keeping ourselves apathetic, lest the extent of our marginality create cognitive dissonance, with our sense of individuality (read "rugged individualism"). The type of identity that seems to require apathy as both a necessary condition as well as a defense mechanism we call "secondary identity." Its opposite is "primary identity."

Primary identity, one formed usually in the context of primary groups and primary relationships, is a core identity that affirms one's existence as a human being. A view of one's sanctity as a human being seems involved here, where one feels fulfilled as a person, and one with his or her community. Here, the individual does not have to justify his existence to himself either through work or the accumulation of wealth and other material goods. Just his "being" in and of itself justifies his existence in his own eyes. He regards himself affectively, particularistically, and diffusely, since his socialization primarily occurs in such a context of primary relationships.

We are concerned here with secondary identity. Here, the individual views himself as a manipulable object. He not only feels constrained but his self is predicated upon who and how many he is able to please. The correlative attitude has been called "other direction."[22] This type of identity may be found in the form of an organizational chart, mobilized by the folded hands of the schoolchild who rather early in the game comes to realize that the teacher rewards discipline far more than he or she does creativity. It is found in the philosophy of the college student that he just puts in four years so that he can attain what he considers to be some measure of financial security. It is found in the philosophy of the graduate student who is willing to put up with all kinds of indignities so that he may become a "doctor." It is found in the philosophy of the faculty member who will keep his mouth shut "until I am promoted and given tenure." It is found in the philosophy of the struggling worker who loudly sings the praises of free enterprise, even if he cannot afford to pay for an operation for his spouse. Secondary identity seems unbiquitous and institutionalized in our society by both apathy and a rigid adherence to belief in our "ideal culture" (what we say exists) rather than in our "real culture" (what actually exists.)

Given the predominance of secondary relationships, identity is up for grabs. It depends upon the type of others with whom one has specific, universalistic, and affectively neutral relations. We have suggested above how identity gives us a vested interest in maintaining our own marginality. It will now be our task to suggest how identity crises, coupled with the constriction of frontiers, gives us a vested interest in maintaining the marginality of others. Marginality serves as a very effective control mechanism. What better way to avoid insults, unpleasant people, or their condition than by constructing boundaries to facilitate their "keeping their distance?" The key to the executive washroom is, therefore, more than a perquisite or accouterment of status. It is a boundary maintaining mechanism insuring the marginality of certain others as well as one's own. More symbolically, titles, such as doctor, professor, Mr., et cetera, may not be terms denoting respect as much as they formalize relationships to insure the marginality of the interactants, which also reinforces one's secondary identity.

If secondary identity yields marginality, and if marginality reinforces secondary identity, we each have a vested interest in keeping ourselves and others marginal to minimize dissonance with our secondary identity which is functional to our basically mobile, organizational, instrumental, way of life. Marginality may not only be seen as a control mechanism, but also as a "frontier." There are very few, if any, frontiers open to the average person in American society today. Horatio Alger stories are quite uncommon. One does not start farming without any capital. Most young people today do not want to own businesses, nor do they find the odds in their favor.[23] Where are the challenges? Where are the frontiers that cement ingroup feelings? It appears that one of the paradoxes of our existence is that we have to create marginality if we are to have some amount of ingroup feeling. This ingroup feeling is instrumentally attained and fills utilitarian functions consonant with the needs of our secondary identity. If there can be said to be one law in sociology it is: when there is a threatening outgroup, the ingroup will unite to defend itself against that threatening outgroup.[24] Marginality seems the major vehicle by which we develop we-group feeling. What cements people of the middle class to each other? What helps maintain their community of interests? It is the creation of outgroups comprised of people who usually have the middle class as a reference group and who are therefore marginal. People cheating on welfare; why don't the poor work and better themselves like we did?; there is no end to the spiraling of taxes. Here, we have a vested interest in creating and maintaining the marginality of others, so that we can establish some small measure of identity beyond that of a manipulable object, so that we can justify our existence. In the 1960's it must have been nothing short of obscene to a man who had trouble making ends meet, to have seen so many young people eschew that kind of life and flaunt seemingly dissonant values in his face. To legitimate much of the past thirty years, the man frequently felt constrained to in turn eschew those dissonant values by imputing negative qualities upon the bearers of those values. Hence, marginality is created and is functional not only as a control mechanism, but also functional as a device to perpetuate middle-class values.

We therefore appear to have a vested interest in being marginal and maintaining the marginality of others. One of the reasons has been stated as the perpetuation of middle-class values. In addition to the above perceived examples, one more may suffice to indicate the prevalence and pervasiveness of this phenomenon before we finally sew this crazy quilt of patches. In most of our dealings with other people we seem to value appearance far more than we do competence. Many books and articles in the general media have been written on "dressing for success" "power ties;" "color coordination to land that job or account." This even is the case when competence would seem to be sorely needed and advantageous. For example, picture a typical man applying for a job. He makes sure he is clean shaven, his hair is cut properly. He is wearing a conservative suit, (if he is applying for a white collar position), and comports himself with mannerly decorum. Should a man applying for a job as an engineer, for example, show up for his interview in dungarees and needing a shave, it is highly questionable whether he would be offered the job, regardless of his credentials, or competence. Appearance is not only a tool of impression management,[25] it is a major way of becoming integrated in or alienated from a reference group. We can easily develop a community with others depending upon how we dress. The worker wears overalls, the doctor wears his "whites", the Shriner wears his fez. These are not only symbols of status, but serve to separate the wearer from others not of that group. The wearer alienates others and is himself alienated. Such alienation as we have seen is functional as both a control mechanism (to keep others at a distance); as a way of reinforcing our secondary identity so that we can more effectively cope in a mobile society primarily made up of secondary relationships as a means of creating ingroups through the creation of outgroups; as a way of perpetuating middle-class values.

The analysis of marginality as an institution in and of itself is interesting. It sheds light on a social phenomenon that is not only significant but quite relevant to all of us in our complex, heterogeneous, industrial society. But the major aim of this discussion has been to set the stage for a discourse on what we have termed "applied sociology," and its role in the general area of sociology. In turn, by discussing the role of sociology as a humanistic discipline in a liberal arts education, we may better view the role of applied sociology as a contribution to that education. Marginality is one institution among others, many of which to some extent also alienate us from others, and serve to place us on the periphery of ongoing activity engaged in by members of our reference group. To analyze marginality in this way does not in and of itself contribute to applied sociology or to the relevance of the analysis to the scholar. What does give it its relevance is its use in awakening consciousness and dispelling false consciousness about one's place in society, so that meaningful alternatives one may use in coping with contingencies of his or her existence are explored to the fullest. This should not only be the role of applied sociology, or of sociology itself,[26] but of a liberal arts education as well.

At the beginning of this chapter the broad outlines of applied sociology were sketched to set the stage for the analysis of marginality as an institution. It will now be our task to use our analysis of marginality as a way of specifying the function of applied sociology for sociology and for a liberal arts education. H. Laurence Ross states: "...A Sociological education can inform students of the nature of social constraint; of the fact that norms, values and beliefs are social in origin rather than biological or physical. It can explain the mechanisms that sustain cultural prescriptions, the relations between culture and personality that result in individuals' bearing the culture without consciousness of this fact. Sociological theory implies that what might be good or functional for the group as a whole may not necessarily be in the best interests of individual members of the group, and that individuals may resist group prescriptions and at times be better off for their resistance. It furthermore implies that deviation can be a source of desirable social change which in the long run may result in greater utility for the majority of the group members. The awareness of social constraints, then, can be said to increase individual freedom, by suggesting that the alternatives for action in consequential situations are greater than previously imagined. ... this potential for individual freedom and rational action is the core of sociology's contribution to the liberal education".[27]

Understanding marginality, therefore, may aid us in developing a community of interests in light of the social constraints that engender and are an outgrowth of that marginality. An additional requisite for awakening consciousness seems to be that we not only view sociology as a "science" but as a "profession." Marginality and its consequences seem to take on more startling proportions when viewed within such a framework.

Sociology may be viewed as a science and profession not only for the sociologist but for the layman as well. How can it be viewed as both a science and a profession? First of all it helps us understand the society we live in. We become acquainted with many different values and beliefs extant in that society many of which may or may not be our own. We learn about many of the institutions of that society, such as family, religious, governmental, economic, and stratification institutions. We learn about certain behaviors some of which are defined as criminal or deviant and why this is so. We also learn that people have vested interests in foisting their values upon others, and institutionalize middle class values in our criminal laws and in our definitions of what is acceptable and not acceptable in our society. We also become acquainted with many social problems in our society and explore their causes and possible solutions in the context of our social structure and its institutions. We also learn about the "mechanics" of our society, such as bureaucracy, methods engendering conformity in society, and methods of challenging the status quo.

Secondly, sociology helps us understand others. We learn about the "stuff" of interaction embodied in our mutuality or reciprocity of expectations. We learn that if interaction is to proceed relatively smoothly, we must be able to quite accurately predict other people's responses to our behavior; they must be able to quite accurately predict our responses to their behavior. We also learn about dilemmas confronting "disadvantaged" people in our society. We learn about being poor in a relatively affluent society; we learn about leisure time in a society to some extent valuing the work ethic. We also learn about personal problems attendant upon the existing configuration of the social structure and its institutions and values. One example is social pressures engendering mental illness.[28]

Thirdly, we also learn that there is a wide range of what we call "normal." Human behavior differs according to one's place in history; one's ideologies, biology (gender, size, and so on), geography, caprice, health, one's status in the class hierarchy, education, happiness, and these and many other qualities in others one confronts everyday.

Finally, sociology helps us understand ourselves. We learn about the process of socialization, or how we become a "self." We learn the mechanics of the development of an identity of self. We also learn about the impingements of our own and other people's values upon us; the impingements of the mechanics and institutions and other social forces upon us and how we confront them and come to terms with them. For example, a major question that sociology seeks to address is: "How does the individual (read "I") become tractable to social controls?" When we come to terms with the answers to this question, we learn that much more about ourselves and about our place and role in the social structure.

Applied sociology is an attempt to realize the promise of sociology as a profession. By making us aware of our community of interests, we take the first step in seeking and effecting solutions to social and personal problems the core of which lie in the social structure. By recognizing that most of us share a common fate of marginality, and the reasons for this fate, derivative grievances may be redressed by mobilizing motivation to change appropriate parts of the social structure. It is the role of applied sociology to not only help mobilize this motivation, but to suggest strategic points in the social structure in which intervention may occur. Finally, the sociologist may, on the basis of his or her knowledge of the social structure, help people alter the social structure to effect the changes they desire. Here, knowledge is put to use in a very real way. We do not become social engineers, but social therapists. We are physicians and society is our patient. If certain people want to solve a problem, and the sociologist also perceives it as a problem, and feels he or she can be of help, he or she makes use of his or her knowledge in redressing the grievances.

Sociology holds out the promise of aiding us in better understanding ourselves, our society and its institutions, and our relationship to those institutions. We may not only use our knowledge in transmitting cultural values, but in altering those values. We do not only become a science, but become a profession. By articulating our expertise in the field we may help our society thrive and aid people in living lives that they feel will be most fulfilling and meaningful for them. In this way we not only pay lip service to the promise of sociology, but elevate the discipline through our service to those we study. Our promise may be realized, people may be helped, our knowledge must be applied. Involved here is a recognition that no problem is beyond solution if motivation is mobilized, and we make full use of our knowledge and courage. What better incentive to study and understand sociology?

NOTES

*A variation of this chapter appeared in my book <u>Essays on Deviance and Marginality</u>, Lanham, Maryland: University Press of America, 1979.

1. C. Wright Mills, <u>The Sociological Imagination</u>, New York: Grove Press, Inc., 1961.

2. Karl Marx, and Frederick Engels, <u>The German Ideology</u>, New York: International Publishers, 1947, pp. 16-17.

3. Leonard Broom and Philip Selznick, <u>Sociology: A Text with Adapted Readings</u>, Evanston, Illinois: Row Peterson and Company, 1960, p. 27.

4. Everett V. Stonequist, <u>The Marginal Man: A Study in Personality and Culture Conflict</u>, New York: Charles C. Scribner's sons, 1937.

5. Emile Durkheim, <u>The Rules of Sociological Method</u>, Chicago: University of Chicago Press, 1938.

6. Who should be "seen and not heard."

7. Edgar Z. Friedenberg, <u>Coming of Age in America</u>, New York: Random House, Inc., 1965.

8. Betty Friedan, <u>The Feminine Mystique</u>, New York: Dell Publishing Company, 1964.

9. Howard S. Becker, <u>Outsiders: Studies in the Sociology of Deviance</u>, New York: The Free Press, 1966.

10. Michael Harrington, <u>The Other America: Poverty in the United States</u>, Baltimore: Penguin Books, 1968.

11. James E. Birren, ed., <u>Handbook of Aging and the Individual</u>, Chicago: University of Chicago Press, 1959.

12. Talcott Parsons, <u>Essays in Sociological Theory</u>, New York: The Free Press of Glencoe, 1954, pp.89-103.

13. Albert K. Cohen, <u>Delinquent Boys: The Culture of the Gang</u>, Glencoe: The Free Press, 1955.

14. George Herbert Mead, <u>Mind, Self and Society: From The Standpoint of a Social Behaviorist,</u> Chicago and London: The University of Chicago Press, 1963.

15. Marshall McLuhan and Quentin Fiore, <u>The Medium is the Message,</u> New York: Random House, 1967.

16. Paul B. Horton and Chester L. Hunt, <u>Sociology,</u> New York: McGraw-Hill Book Company, 1968., p.278.

17. Eugene Litwak, "Occupational Mobility and Extended Family Cohesion", <u>ASR,</u> 25, February, 1960, pp 9-21; "Geographic Mobility and Extended Family Cohesion", <u>ASR</u>, 25, June, 1960, pp. 385-394.

18. Leonard Broom and Philip Selznick, <u>op. cit.,</u> pp. 124-127.

19. Talcott Parsons and Edward A. Shils, eds., <u>Toward a General Theory of Action: Theoretical Foundations for the Social Sciences,</u> New York and Evanston: Harper and Row, Publishers, 1962, pp. 76-88.

20. <u>Ibid.</u>

21. Leon Festinger, Henry W. Rieken, and Stanley Schacter, <u>When Prophecy Fails,</u> Minneapolis: University of Minneapolis Press, 1956.

22. David Riesman, Nathan Glazer, and Reuel Denney, <u>The Lonely Crowd: A Study of the Changing American Character,</u> Garden City, New York: Doubleday Anchor Books, 1953, pp.34-38.

23. C. Wright Mills, <u>White Collar: The American Middle Classes,</u> New York: Oxford University Press, 1956, 1953, pp. 63-68.

24. Muzafer Sherif, "Experiments in Group Conflict" <u>Scientific American</u>, 195, 1956, pp. 54-58.

25. Erving Goffman, <u>The Presentation of Self in Everyday Life</u>, Garden City: Doubleday and Company, Inc., 1959, pp. 208-237. For a more detailed analysis of the role of appearance in analyzing impressions see Erving Goffman, <u>Stigma: Notes on the Management of Spoiled Identity,</u> Englewood Cliffs, New Jersey; Prentice-Hall, Inc., 1964.

26. See H. Laurence Ross, "The Teaching of Sociology In the Metropolitan College," <u>The American Sociologist</u>, 1, May, 1966, pp. 143-144.

27. <u>Ibid.</u>, p. 143.

28.   See, for example, August B. Hollingshead and Frederick Redlich, "Social Stratification and Psychiatric Disorders," <u>American Sociological Review</u>, 18, April, 1953, pp. 153-169.

Chapter Two

Some Consequences of
Educational Socialization*

In (the movie) <u>The Graduate,</u> as in upper middle-class America
generally, parents relate to their children in a somewhat vampiresque way.
They feed on the child's accomplishments, sucking sustenance for their
pale lives from vicarious enjoyment of his or her development. In a
sense, this sucking is appropriate since the parents give so much--lavish
so much care, love, thoughtfulness, and self-sacrifice on their blood bank.
But this is little comfort for the child, who at some point must rise above
his guilt and live his own life--the culture demands it of him. And, after
all, a vampire is a vampire.[1]

In his perceptive book, Philip Slater here calls attention to what we may call
"institutionalized vampirism" endemic, not only in middle-class America, but
within much of civilization as a whole. Such institutionalized vampirism may
be seen in many phases of one's life: the family, the work situation, the
economic structure, etc. However, this vampirism may be seen most readily
and, indeed, poignantly within schools; its existence not only describes various
attendant phenomena, such as "alienation" and "apathy" but may be seen to go a
long way toward explaining the rather harsh realities of much of the barrenness
of "the intellectual life." Just as the reality shock many people experience upon
entering academic life is profound, so is the impact of "anti-intellectualism" with
the academy. There has always been a history of such anti-intellectualism in our
country, but only within the past two decades does it seem to have taken root
within the ivory tower stronghold that had hitherto acted as a buffer and
protection for the academic against this onslaught.

The major purpose of this chapter is to seek to explain seeming "alienation"
and "apathy" among students, the underpinnings of which may be seen to lie a
thinly veiled, and not too well disguised contempt for the academic life. (I don't
believe we are important enough as academics in the students' lives to be

deserving of their hostility.) Moreover, the reality shocks many of us have upon establishing a career in academia may also be partly explained via the vehicle of institutionalized vampirism.   That the existence of this vampirism within graduate school life (which will be the focus of this chapter) is not obvious to all of us, may I think be in part accounted for by the "mystification of experience,"[2] that is so important to the socialization of the future academic. The basis of that socialization, and its relationship to the realities of "the intellectual life" will now be explored.

To mystify an experience is to make it into what it is not. Through the alchemy of mystification one is taught to view a negative experience as being "positive" or at least justifiable. As Laing says: "Children are not yet fools, but we shall turn them into imbeciles like ourselves, with high I.Q.',s if possible."[3] We mystify the robotization of our students and through the magic of alchemy transform our perception of it (and frequently even their perception of it) as being necessary, just and even rewarding. When the alchemy does not affect their perception, however, and when the students are not convinced that their best interests are being served by the academy and its functionaries, their "rebellion" frequently takes the form of compulsive docility, seeming inability to become interested in ideas, an inability to grasp abstractions of even the simplest nature. We dislike their brutishness, for, I suggest, within that brutishness we see ourselves--and we see ourselves as we were as graduate students.

To seek to understand the underpinnings of the "institutionalized vampirism" and the "mystification of experience" that occurs in graduate school, I would like to discuss the processes, content, outcomes, and prospects of graduate school socialization. One of the most salient features of the graduate school experience seems to be its "irrationality." In professional schools such as those dealing with law, medicine, dentistry, and so forth, there may be seen to be a predictable career (or predictable sequence of steps) one goes through for a specified number of years. In these schools the student knows that in one year he will be in the shoes of the person who is now one year ahead of him, should he be able to master the subjects that he is now taking. There is a sense not only of an integrated order, but also a sense of "progress as one moves from one step to the next. In graduate school on the other hand this is not usually the case. In Sociology, for example, it is viewed as a "horizontal" rather than a "vertical" discipline. In the latter case, one course presupposes knowledge of another course, as is usual in the aforementioned types of school. However, Sociology is viewed as a perspective, the acquiring of which need not be done in any particular sequence or serial order. Indeed, there does not seem to be such a regular sequence established. This being the case, not only is there little inherent order, but little sense of "progress," and, hence, no predictable career.

Coupled with the lack of a predictable career is the further "irrationality" of the thesis. By irrationality in this context is meant no clear or even necessary connection between means and ends. The fostered dependence upon "advisors" who carefully examine every word, whose likes and dislikes, biases and preferences must be known and adhered to by the student is the reality of the trauma of the dissertation. Ideas do not seem to be as important as the judicious interpretation of data; the long view and the perspective on the subject do not seem to be as important as the survey of literature (the accuracy of which is hardly at issue); the love of learning is not at all relevant--or certainly not as relevant as the laborious process of revising one's way into the academic fraternity. Moreover, the word "advisor" may be seen as a euphemism. In reality he frequently becomes the unpredictable policeman who fondles his club without necessarily striking one with it--although the injunction is clear that he may, and that he has, and that he can. Academic life is filled with horror stories of graduate students thinking that they had come to the end of their graduate school career, only to have their "advisors" tell them that their questionnaire had to be reworded, new data had to be obtained, etc. This element of irrationality bespeaks not only institutionalized vampirism, but a cruelty of a most unspeakable nature.

Mystification of these experiences notwithstanding, these horror stories are not isolated occurrences but seem to occur relatively frequently. Their occurrence, moreover, does not stem from evil people using dependent students to fill their ego needs. Their occurrence is institutionalized within the educational institution and is part and parcel of the reality of everyday life of the student within it. Creativity is risky in these leagues; docility and conventionality are more frequently and regularly rewarded. What creativity that is likely to occur occurs within the narrow framework of the advisor's prejudices and the most conventional literature and studies done in the given field. Moreover, the utmost in creativity is institutionally encouraged not in reference to the subject matter, but in reference to the playing of the role perceived as acceptable to one's "advisor." The mystification of the graduate school experience comes full circle when the student successfully introjects the roles and biases of his advisor and the other "relevant" faculty who hold the club over his career and life chances to the point where he actually comes to see the rationality of their actions and perceptions. The near panic reaction of the carpet being pulled from under the student who has committed several years to a goal that can be snatched from him with no more than a cursory acknowledgment, and with no possibility of redress, becomes transformed upon the awarding of the degree to a conventionalized narcissism, not of the intellectual or physical self, but of the "academic" trappings that represent the most conventional values both of the academy and of the middle-class society in which one lives. With this stance, "form" becomes more important than "content." This is not only true of the thesis, but of the relationship of the student to his advisor.

Although the form may be at least as important as the content of the processes of socialization of the graduate student, there are some telling aspects of the content that seem worth exploring. Coupled with the "irrationality" of the curriculum, it is very rare in just my experience that the graduate student receives less than a "B" in a course, frequently and usually independently of his performance. Since a "B" average is required, most instructors have an unwritten code of giving a "B" except in unusual circumstances. Therefore, not only is the eventual outcome of career contingencies (the awarding or not of the degree) to a great degree independent of content (or performance, or grade) but the grade itself is also to a great degree independent of such performance.

The narrow, irrelevant, punishing thesis sets the tone of the hazing ceremony that is part and parcel of the initiation of the student into the academic fraternity. However, the content of this aspect of socialization suggests to the student that a contribution to knowledge (which, through the mystification of experience, a dissertation is supposed to represent) and knowledge itself is similarly punishing and relatively dull. In the dissertation, the hypotheses are narrow, frequently divorced (or made to be divorced) from the real world, and also frequently divorced from substantive theory. Thus, the relationship of data to theory, analysis to interpretation, and the intellectual life to life itself, appears strongly and awesomely remote. Yet, through the mystification of the experience, we obtain the results of this socialization--and we obtain them with a vengeance. Some of these negative results may be enumerated as follows: (1) the "Getting Even Syndrome." Here, the professor, perhaps unwittingly, seeks to get back at his own students to make them go through what he did or at least have them appreciate what he had to go through. As Farber[4] points out, the professor thus makes his accomplishments seem awesomely remote from the possible grasp of the student.
(2)The "Subversion of Scholarship." For many professors, the last research they do is the dissertation. If they do further research it is frequently mandated for their tenure and promotion. As an acquaintance of mine said, many of these publications are meant to be indexed rather than read. (3) Within the academic profession, there is the encouragement of docility and "safe" people, both intellectually and politically safe. Many examples have been related to me of people who were refused academic appointments because of their political involvements. (4) The encouragement of the retreat into bureaucracy--and a reliance upon that bureaucracy for upward mobility. This desire for upward mobility, so much a part of our culture is frequently antithetical to a life of scholarship--where one follows his or her muse and stands by his or her convictions regardless of the consequences. (5) The encouragement of timidity results both in the "getting even syndrome" and the opposite syndrome which embodies the pandering after student approval. It may be seen that such things as student evaluations of faculty increase this timidity and make the professor pander after student approval, not only for ego needs but for career and life-chance needs.

Given the nature of educational socialization, here depicted in graduate school, the harvesting of the above results have been obtained and will be increasingly obtained in the future. Some of these prospects may be seen as follows: (1) There will be increased bureaucratic controls over the seemingly hitherto professional aspects of our work (although the idea of professionalism may too have been a result of the mystification of experience, and the bureaucratization may be a function of demystification). With a tighter job market, with the supply exceeding the demand, we may expect bureaucratic controls to increase proportionately. (2) The notion of "career" will be replaced by "job," and each will be expendable. Docility and timidity inveigh against the ready acceptance of unionism or professionalism, to protect the academic worker. In the absence of severe union controls, what counter-measures occur will be of the most timid, half-hearted sort. (3) As form replaces content in priority, quantity will replace quality. Increasingly, the number of articles written and the number of papers delivered will be considered more important than the quality of these products. In the teaching area, an eight to five routine may become mandatory, with a panel choosing the textbooks, deciding the amount and type of material to be covered in a course, etc. (4) Lastly, and perhaps most importantly, the aesthetic dimensions of our work (another mystification?) which cannot be measured, and to measure them does them violence, will be replaced by the equivalent of the McGuffy reader. What is not quantifiable for the politicians and cost accountants will not be allowed.

We have built an educational edifice of profound proportions. The coordination of quite complex tasks necessary to administer that edifice is actually staggering. But again, our penchant for form has held sway over our concern for content. In this case, the content of the subject matter need not be examined, but the content of what has been done to us and what we in turn are doing to our students, must be fully explored. We can mystify these relationships and blissfully carry on, but we can expect that we will increasingly pay the price of such mystification. The person we "turn out," as the person we have turned out to be, and the relationship of each to the other, is certainly deserving of more exploration. To do otherwise may reap a whirlwind which few of us would like to see and from which few of us would be able to profit.

NOTES

*Text of a paper read at meetings of the Community College Social Science Association, November 2-4, 1972, and appears in the Community College Social Science Quarterly, Fall, 1973. A variation of this chapter also appeared in my book Essays of Deviance and Marginality, Lanham, Maryland: University Press of America, 1979.

1. Philip Slater, The Pursuit of Loneliness: American Culture at the Breaking Point, Boston: Beacon Press, 1972, p. 59.

2. R.D. Laing, The Politics of Experience, New York: Ballantine Books, 1968, pp. 57-76.

3. Ibid., p. 58.

4. Jerry Farber, The Student as Nigger: Essay and Stories, North Hollywood, California: Contact Books, 1969, p. 122.

Chapter Three

Work and Political Conservatism*

H.F. Harlow did a number of experiments where monkeys were raised not by real mothers but by surrogate mothers that were wire dummies covered with terrycloth. During infancy the monkeys formed strong attachments to these terrycloth surrogates but when they reached maturity both their capacity for reproduction and for rearing their own young was minimal. They were deficient in experience about mothering, which has often been thought to be instinctual.[1]

Introduction

One of the main purposes of this chapter is to try to explain the political conservatism of the lower, working, and middle classes. Sociologists have been confronted with some embarrassing phenomena that we have usually met by ignoring. Marxists, and many social scientists, have sought to explain arch conservatism among much of the working class by utilizing the Marxian concept of "false consciousness." This occurred, despite the injunctions of the sociology of knowledge and the existential argument. Rather than seeing man as having choice in a finitely structured situation, we have been very quick to promulgate the notions of "false consciousness" and "structural constraint" to explain such conservatism. These concepts may be seen to very superficially explain the phenomenon but do more to "describe" the political orientation and world view of the working classes. "Structural Constraint" may help explain mere acceptance of rules and injunctions (as if there is anything mere about acceptance) but does not seem to do justice to the relatively tenacious embracing of these rules and injunctions. When such embracing behavior is rationalized (away) by middle-class sociologists, their theories may be seen to be due more to their imputation of their own rationalities and categories of thought upon other people than to the amount of variance regarding such embracing behavior that seems to be accounted for by such notions as "false consciousness" and "structural constraint."

To try to explain "embracing behavior," even under conditions that do not seem rational to middle-class sociologists, we have to go into the biological infrastructure of man and the relationship between his libidinal drives and the routinized power relationships (Weber's notion of "authority"[2]) found in the most pervasive aspect of his life: his work. There may be seen to be an emotional and aesthetic (erotic) cathexis between the individual and his work that should go a long way in accounting for the embracing behavior we are about to describe.

The Derivation of the Proposition

Both Ludwig Feuerbach and the young Marx saw alienation as the destruction of sexuality. "...the alienated man was one who had acquired a horror of his sexual life, and whose whole way of thinking was determined by this repression of sexuality.[3] The alienation of man from himself signified that his natural human emotions had been distorted. 'Alienation signified a mode of life in which man was being compelled by social circumstances to act self destructively,' to cooperate in his own self-mutilation, his castration, that is, the destruction of his own manhood. The economy that men had created presumably to satisfy their needs was finally warping their deepest instincts. Repeatedly the young Marx and Engels characterized the bourgeois society in metaphors and actualities of sexual alienation. Economic exploitation eventuated in the mutilations of sexual alienation."[4]

The derivation of the notion of "alienation" presupposes a philosophical stance very much a part of Western civilization: the inner _versus_ the outer; the internal _versus_ the external; the individual _versus_ the environment; the self _versus_ the other. Indeed, Freud lent further credence to this philosophical stance, most notably in his book Civilization and Its Discontents.[5] Freud felt that, through the "reality principle," the needs of civilization demanded repression of man's drives. Man's drives (his libido) were seen as inherently antithetical to the requirements of civilization, not only regarding the enhancement of predictability of behavior, but also to enable the harnessing of the sexual drive and redirecting it to do the "necessary work" of society. Superego structures are thus created via the scaffolding of guilt feelings. Internalized controls thus supplement external controls, so that power relations are not only institutionalized, but legitimated through a moral compulsion to obey by the individual. Man's socialization is to this extent biological, and to help explain his responses to rules and injunctions the libidinal underpinnings of such conforming and embracing behavior will have to be explored.

In social theory perhaps Herbert Marcuse comes closet to grappling with this problem. Rather than rely on the historical notion of Freud's "reality principle", which opposes the libidinal needs of the "pleasure principle," Marcuse uses the historically specific notion of "performance principle" which only opposes or need oppose the pleasure principle within a given historical epoch. The basic variable determining and necessitating such opposition and repression is economic. Freud states that society's motive in repressing the instinctual structure is "economic; since it has not means enough to support life for its members without work on their part, it must see to it that the number of these members is restricted and their energies directed away from sexual activities on to their work."[6] Marcuse agrees but sees justification for repression given a scarcity of goods and services to the extent that the perpetuation of the species is threatened. However, when such conditions are absent, such conditions of repression he calls "surplus repression."[7] In other words, he feels that a non-repressive civilization, giving free play to the aesthetic, erotic mode, is possible. He envisions such a society as follows: when society has reached the stage where there is no longer a struggle for existence, and where work has been replaced by play, and the performance principle by contemplation and display (civilized narcissism) a set of basic transformations follows: "The body in it entirety would become an object of cathexis, a thing to be enjoyed -- an instrument of pleasure. This change in the value and scope of libidinal relations would lead to a disintegration of the institutions in which the private interpersonal relations have been organized, particularly the monogamic and patriarchal drive. The pleasure principle reveals its own dialectic. The erotic aim of sustaining the entire body as subject-object of pleasure calls for internal refinement of the organism, the intensification of its receptivity, the growth of its sensuousness...."[9]

At least two questions can be leveled at Marcuse's conclusions: (1) Why assume that work--even "alienated labor"--is external to the individual? (2) Why assume that the eroticization of modern man can take place in the absence of work? History may be dialectical, but there may be memory traces that direct and focus libidinal drives. If work is a central life interest for a great period of time, as with the terrycloth mother, it may become one of the few appropriate objects of eroticization. As Lyman and Scott have observed: "Certain groups are spatially deprived of free territory--that is the ecological conditions that afford opportunities of idiosyncrasy and expression of desired identities." There frequently results various kinds of body manipulation, body adornment and body penetration: the modification of inner space.[10] They suggest a hypothesis "that as other forms of free territory are perceived to be foreclosed by certain segments of the society, these segments...will utilize more frequently and intensively the area of body space as a free territory.[11] Work itself may also be seen to be an object of eroticization via such libidinal cathexis. If work is a central life interest for most people,[12] and if it voluntarily or involuntarily pervades most of one's waking hours, and if sexuality is of sufficient importance that it is "the only function of a living organism which extends beyond the individual and secures its connection with its species" then if cognitive dissonance is to be minimized, and if a schizophrenic split between different levels of reality is to be mediated, work must provide some avenue for channeling this sexuality. In fact, Freud suggested such a possibility by saying that work provides an opportunity for a "very considerable discharge of libidinal component impulses, narcissistic, aggressive and erotic.[13] Ives Hendrick was even more direct, in that he felt that work, because it was the gratification of an instinct, yielded pleasure in its efficient performance. In this sense, work pleasure and libidinal pleasure usually coincide since work serves as an outlet for the discharge of surplus libidinal tension.[14]

Indeed, this seems to be the philosophical assumption that Freud used when viewing sexuality as harnessed and redirected to do the necessary work of civilization. Is it all that preposterous, then, to see that sexuality, not only implicated in the work situation, but as a very vital part of that situation? To the degree that work cannot exist without the harnessing sexuality, it may be seen that it is to that degree that there is a libidinal cathexis with the work itself. Such cathexis may be seen to be part and parcel of the sexualization of commodities and the occupational attitudes toward sex. Some examples of such phenomena will follow. In describing the sexualization of commodities, Philip Slater states: "The act of buying has become so sexualized in our society that packaging has become a major industry: we must even wrap a small purchase before carrying it from the store to our home. Carrying naked purchases down the street in broad daylight seems indecent to Americans (Europeans can still do it but are becoming increasingly uneasy as advertising in Europe become more sexualized). After all, if we are induced to buy something because of the erotic delights that are covertly promised with it, then buying becomes a sexual act. Indeed, we are approaching the point where it absorbs more sexual interest than sex itself. When this happens people will be more comfortable walking in the street nude than with an unwrapped purchase. Package modesty has increased in direct proportion as body modesty has lessened."[15]

In describing the occupationalization of sex, Lewis and Brissett show that sex manuals portray sexual activity as work. Indeed, there are seen to be work schedules, techniques, considerable effort required, et cetera. They suggest that this phenomenon may be due to our need to justify and dignify play. They state that this is not disguising man's play as work: his play has in fact become work.[16]

Such examples point out the eroticization of commodities, and the occupationalization of sexual activity. Psychoanalytic theory, moreover, has set the foundations for the analysis of the eroticization of work, as seen above.

In discussing and analyzing the relationship between man and his work, the dualities of internal versus external, man versus environment, etc., may be inappropriate and merely a function of the rationalities of middle-class intellectuals and laymen, in mid-twentieth century western civilization. Rather than there being a duality between man and his work, there may be seen to be an identity between the two, not merely because of one's acquired concept of self, economic needs, or social-emotional legitimation in corporate society, but because of libidinal cathexis. When sexuality was harnessed for the necessary work of civilization, a Frankenstein's monster was created, whereby the work itself became at least as much an object of sexuality as more traditional objects.

In this connection, the notion of "alienation" may not only be a result of these middle class rationalities, but only in a most superficial way describe the relationship between man and his work. Moreover, the notion of alienation may be generated more from socially legitimate responses than from the phenomenological underpinnings which underlie and are masked by such rationalities and responses. Statements such as the reporting that both alienation from work and alienation from expressive relations are found to be more prominent in highly centralized and highly formalized organizations,[17] and that even middle-class people increasingly "work at jobs which are routinzed and specialized and over which they exercise little or no control,"[18] misses the point of libidinal cathexis. Such notions revolving around the supposed alienation or estrangement of man from his work may very well reflect the dualities inherent in our current view of the world, and do not do justice to alternative explanations of man's relationship to his work, mediated particularly by the rules and injunctions which most sociologists mistakenly relate with what I feel to be the inappropriate and, to a great degree, inaccurate notion of "alienation." As Marcuse states,[19] technological forces "deliver the goods" to people, and insofar as their needs (whether true or false)[20] are not revolutionary, activity against the relations of production fulfilling those needs would be not only irrational, but from my point of view, impossible.

The extent to which man not merely accepts his work, and the necessity of work itself, but embraces that work, its felt necessity and the social control mechanisms of rules and injunctions that are part and parcel of that work, it is to that extent that we may see the aftermath of the harnessing of sexuality in work. That aftermath may be seen to be a libidinal cathexis to that work, to the extent that erotic gratifications are received by the work itself. Such gratifications may be seen to be not merely a by-product of the work, but a justification for engaging in the work in the first place. To derive such erotic gratification is a function of socializing influences both on and off the job, perhaps from memory traces from a time in civilization where the harnessing of the sexual drive was crucial to the survival of the species, perhaps from the delights realized from the fusion of self and work, mind and action. The conservatism evinced by the working class, the tenacious adherence to the mechanics and way of life that middle-class intellectuals, through their own rationalities view as "alienating," can, I believe, in great part be explained by such a libidinal cathexis with work itself. The dynamics of such a cathexis will now be explored.

The Dynamics of Libidinal Transference

I have tried to show that such notions as "structural constraints" and "alienation" do not do justice to the relationship between man and his work, and may be more a function of the projection of the frustrations of middle-class intellectuals in mid-twentieth century western civilization than an actual analysis of that relationship. In the traditional sociological view, the individual, and particularly the individual as a worker, is treated as the dependent variable who, through external control and the forces of socialization, merely accepts the rules and injunctions embodied in his work, and also merely accepts the necessity of his working in the first place. Through our notion of libidinal cathexis, via the mechanics of libidinal transference (to be discussed below), the voluntaristic dimension of individual choice and action is given much more weight. The individual is not merely a recipient, he more or less consciously chooses; the individual does not merely accept, he more or less consciously embraces.

In a book review I wrote, I stated the voluntaristic dimensions of what we are now calling libidinal cathexis in the following way: "The student to the teacher; the employee to the employer; the Army recruit to the officer; no less than the lover to the beloved may be considered to embrace willing enslavement for the pleasure that such enslavement provides. Power, prestige, wealth, and security, no less than love, may serve as the necessary and sufficient criteria for such enslavement. Such an individual is not necessarily apathetic, as expressed in the popular literature. He is, on the other hand, very much involved and committed to his enslavement, since it is mainly through such a sado-masochistic pose that he may reap what are to him the accouterments of success."[21] This pose is not a put-on for purposes of impression management, but is an actual relationship sociologically and phenomenologically dictated by certain libidinal realities. Beyond the contingencies of socialization, memory traces (both ontogenetic and phylogenetic) , and the rewards of the fusion of feeling and being, thought and action, lies work as an object of libidinal cathexis and transference due to its physical and psychological salience to the individual, in great part created by civilizational needs for the harnessing of sexuality.

The mechanics by which libidinal transference occurs toward work as its object of cathexis, which in turn creates the embracing behavior discussed above, may be enumerated as follows: (1) Man has drives, and these drives comprise Freud's notion of "libido," (2) Man has a finite amount of libidinal energy. (3) Man has to externalize this energy, for to solely internalize it would do direct biological damage to the organism. (4) Man seeks an object for the direction of his energy. This is the stage of libidinal cathexis. (5) The object he chooses may be historically and spatially specific (as occurred with the terry cloth mother surrogate in Harlow's experiment), and is to a great degree dependent upon its salience to him (involving the amount of time he spends with "it," and its frequency and duration in his consciousness. (6) when there is an excess of definitions favorable to the adoption of the object as an appropriate one for the libidinal cathexis as opposed to another object, such cathexis, even if of a temporary nature, is for the time being complete.[22] (7) When the energy is directed from a culturally approved source and an object grounded in the routine, everyday life of people, toward such an object of salience for the individual, libidinal transference has taken place.

Through such a libidinal transference, traditional objects of eroticism are supplemented by other objects, not so well recognized or sanctioned in the realm of everyday life. But such a lack of sanction in the ideal culture does not deny its phenomenological existence or its sociological significance. In contrast to Marcuse, I am suggesting that the aesthetic mode, which allows the play of orphic and narcissistic images and norms, coupled with the rational requisites of civilization, already exists. These are not dimensions to be sought, as a counterforce to supposed Promethean culture heroes[23] who extol the virtues of "toil, productivity and progress,"[24] but are modes of acting and reacting to the realities of work that not only make that work possible, but make it meaningful and "enjoyable." Denials, and the logic of everyday life to the contrary, the tenacious embracing of Prometheus transforms him into an Orphic-Narcissistic image, in which one finds not only his work, but himself as well.

NOTES

*A variation of this chapter appeared in my book Essays on Deviance and Marginality, Lanham, Maryland: University Press of America, 1979.

1. H. F. Harlow, "The Heterosexual Affectional System in Monkeys," American Psychologist, 17, 1962, pp. 1-9.

2. Talcott Parsons, ed., The Theory of Social and Economic Organization, New York: The Free Press, 1957, p. 328.

3. Lewis S. Feuer, Marx and the Intellectuals: A Set of Post Ideological Essays, New York: Doubleday and Company, Inc., 1969, p. 74.

4. Ibid., pp. 75-76.

5. Sigmund Freud, Civilization and Its Discontents, London: Hogarth Press, 1949.

6. Sigmund Freud, A General Introduction to Psychoanalysis, New York: Garden City Publishing Company, 1943, p. 273.

7. Herbert Marcuse, Eros and Civilization: A Philosophical Inquiry into Freud, New York; Vintage Books, 1962, p. 32.

8. Ibid., p. 184.

9. Ibid., p. 193.

10. Stanford Lyman and Marvin B. Scott, "Territoriality: A Neglected Sociological Dimension," Social Problems, Fall, 1967, Vol 15, pp. 236-249.

11. Ibid., p. 248.

12. Sigmund Freud, A General Introduction to Psychoanalysis, op cit., p. 385.

13. Sigmund Freud, Civilizations and Its Discontents, op. cit., p. 34.

14. Herbert Marcuse, Eros and Civilization, op cit., p. 200.

15. Philip Slater, The Pursuit of Loneliness: American Culture at the Breaking Point, Boston Beacon Press, 1970, p. 94.

16. Lionel S. Lewis and Dennis Brissett, "Sex as Work: A Study of Avocational Counseling," Social Problems, Summer, 1967, Vol. 15, pp. 8-18.

17. Michael Aiken and Jerold Hage, "Organizational Alienation: A Comparative Analysis," American Sociological Review, August, 1966, Vol. 31, pp. 497-507.

18. James W. Rinehart, "Affluence and the Embourgeoisement of the Working Class: A Critical Look," Social Problems, Fall, 1971, Vol. 19, p. 159.

19. Herbert Marcuse, One Dimensional Man: Studies in the Ideology of Advanced Industrial Society, Boston, Beacon Press, 1966.

20. In this connection, who is Marcuse or anyone else to label certain needs, whether manipulated or imposed upon others or not, as false. He too, is a product of his social class and its rationalities--"false" rationalities imposed upon others, no more or less false than the needs he argues against.

21. Jerry S. Maneker, A Book Review of the Story of O, by Pauline Reage, (New York: Grove Press, 1967) Indian sociological Bulletin, June, 1969.

22. This statement is loosely borrowed from Edwin Sutherland's theory of Differential Association. See Edwin H. Sutherland and Donald R. Cressey, Principles of Criminology, Philadelphia and New York: J.B. Lippincott Company, 1966, pp. 81-82.

23. Herbert Marcuse, Eros and Civilization, op cit., pp. 144-179.

24. Ibid., p. 146.

Chapter Four

Madness At Work*

The Productivity of Madness

If our reach should exceed our grasp, perhaps contemplation and residence in other than taken-for-granted realities is a noble endeavor. Such a voluntary or involuntary endeavor might more humanely be witnessed with awe rather than derision; viewed as laudable rather than "sick"; treated with respect rather than "treated." In pragmatic, materialistic culture, alternative views of aberrant behavior are not given much credence. Yet our medical view of insanity or madness fits in quite well with our production-oriented society, geared to producing producers and consuming consumers. The producers we produce may safely produce ideas; even those ideas should be production oriented. To produce realms of unfamiliar images might be tolerated under certain specific circumstances (for example, among some poets or artists). However, to live in these realms is expressly forbidden and, indeed, punished in the name of therapy and even humanitarianism.

In some so-called primitive societies dwelling in such unfamiliar houses exalts one to the status of priest or shaman. In other societies, the warmth of the extended family or shelter of a benign community can help soothe the sometimes awesome fear of the dweller. However, in a society such as ours, where productive (or even unproductive) work is a virtue, where money creates power and prestige, and where goods and services can only be bought, the insane are quite useful. Indeed, it seems we need our insane. They, too, are big business--they provide money for all sorts of people who treat them, who house them, and who control them. We also need them to show us who we are, in that they provide us with visible evidence of our constructions of whom we are not like. One can easily see many of them among the homeless, living on the street, which further distances "them" from "us." Their role becomes increasingly important as increasing social change and our own personal dislocations resulting from the distress of painful adaptations cause us to question who we are. There can't be an "us" to question who we are. There can't be an "us" without a "them." We've done this with criminals, with homosexuals, with beatniks, with hippies, with junkies--why not with the insane?

Our values, ideas, and ideologies are frequently social constructions.[2] These constructions meet the needs we have in adapting and readapting, our constructions are changing to meet these needs and make painful dislocations and adaptations plausible and palatable for us. In this way, our lives have some semblance of meaning and what might have been a shattered sense of self is miraculously restored. The mosaic is partially rebuilt by our insane and other "deviants," and our own fear is the cement that holds the construction together. Indeed, it may therefore be seen that we create what we fear, and fear what we create.

One may neither safely generalize about so-called sane behavior nor about so-called insane behavior, and to attempt to do so would be unproductive. However, one thing that category of behaviors called "insane" have in common is that they have all been officially labeled as such. Moreover, this label is the product of a judgment made by people with certain values and fairly fixed ideas of what constitute normality and abnormality. As R. D Laing has said, hundred of millions of "normal" people have in the past fifty years killed hundreds of millions of other normal people.[3] In war, such behavior is laudable. It is therefore not only the given behavior that determines whether the label of "normal" or "abnormal" will be placed, but also how representatives of the dominant value system of our society will react to the given behavior.[4] There seem to be two major criteria that determine such reactions: social class of the subject, and the situation in which the behavior occurs. Money may not buy happiness, but it does by relative insulation from labels. Here, the eccentricities of the wealthy person become the psychoses of the poor. It is no accident that a disproportionate number of lower class people (and undoubtedly, by extension, other people who are also alienated from the decision-making process concerning their own lives) are labeled "psychotic," and populate our state mental hospitals.[5] Were I to read a paper to you at a professional meeting my behavior would be viewed one way; were I to read the paper at a New Year's Eve party, it would mean something else to you. So, it is not only my behavior that is at issue, but the situation in which I engage in the behavior. Our label of "Insane" or "deviant" is a product of behavior in a given situation and what certain influential people choose to do about it. If there were something inherently "insane" about given behaviors, all of us might be successfully tagged with that label.

Paranoia?

On the door of my office, my secretary once taped a poster that read, "Just because you're paranoid, doesn't mean they're not out to get you." Most people would agree that paranoia is one form of so-called aberrant behavior. In a society that is production oriented and requires obedience to its attributions and conformity to its injunctions, paranoia as conventionally defined is not functional and hence not appropriate. The heightened sensitivity of the paranoid if taken seriously might prove embarrassing. For example, let us assume that our subject is deathly afraid of going to work because he feels that he will be killed in the process. His vivid imagination has constructed a scenario that is paralyzing in its totality (much like the scenario we construct of the paranoid). But if we briefly examine this particular example, the paranoia may not seem all that inappropriate. In our society, if a person does not work he or she starves and goes without certain essential goods and services and so do their families, despite food stamps and welfare. If one doesn't work (or have his money work for him), he is at the mercy of a whole host of contingencies and agencies which can either provide or withhold necessary goods and services. When a person imagines such vulnerability attendant upon loss of control over his life and destiny, work takes on a new meaning. An increasing reserve army of labor ready to take that person's job, even if it is minimum wage with no benefits, adds further rationale to that vulnerability. Awesome fear of going to work perhaps becomes more understandable.

When this realization is coupled with the ethics of individuality and competition that are so entrenched in our way of life, so that organizational games of one-upmanship and other forms of backstabbing are salient realities in the working world, an awesome fear of going to work becomes even further understandable. Indeed, if we were going to impose labels on people, those who blithely go off to work in the morning and even enjoy work under conditions described above may be seen to have some dysfunction of reason or sensation. It may be these people who are far more dangerous and destructive in their behavior than are most paranoids. It is the former group who can talk of "looking out for number one," speak unemotionally about the homeless (and about most other things) and who have suspended judgment and affect regarding events that many poets, mystics, artists, scholars and paranoids feel quite keenly and painfully.

My attempt here is not to delve into the nature of paranoia, but to try to demonstrate how our values and institutions of our society determine what types of behaviors we can choose to reward and punish. Moreover, behavior may be seen as a "rational" adaptation to one's environment. One will engage in behavior that has been reinforced either through direct gratification or through some form of recognition. Should there be an absence of such gratification or recognition (either through positive or even negative stroking)[6] the individual might create or discover other worlds more to his or her liking, much as we have created our own.

Our society seems ripe for labels of pathology, for many aspects of our society may be viewed as pathological. The gap between our "ideal culture" (what we say exists) and our "real culture" (what adults learn "really" exists) is so great that guilt puts a blanket on anger. With our Puritan Ethic, guilt is a far more permissible response to the gap than is anger. (Imagine what happens to suppressed rage?) Indeed, guilt's blanket is quite effective for our society in which "adjustment" is such a cherished value. When individuality, competition, and adjustment are extolled as virtues, anger (and some economically non-productive manifestations of guilt) is not only deemed inappropriate but frequently "sick" and "dangerous" as well. The scenario is further mystified by agencies of welfare dedicated to furthering these values in the name of "help" and adjustment. As Sartre has written of Jean Genet, outlaw and playwright: "of course, he is neither cold nor hungry. He is given board and lodging. But there's the rub--he is given them. This child has had more than enough of gifts. Everything is a gift, including the air he breathes. He has to say 'thank you' for everything. Every minute a gift is put into his hands at the whim of a generosity that leaves its mark on him forever. Every minute Genet moves a little further away from his foster parents. All this bounty obliges him to recognize that they were not obliged to adopt him, to feed him, to take care of him; that they 'owed him nothing,' that he is obliged to them, that they were quite free not to give him what he was not free to accept, in short, that he is not their son. A true son does not have to display his gratitude. He draws from the family purse, and it is his father's duty to bring him up. Deprived of everything through the kindness of others, Genet will later express his hatred of all generosity toward inferiors..."[7] In a society such as ours, conventional sanity is not necessarily a gift and what may be the gift of insanity is not allowed to be cherished. and all this in the name of humaneness and treatment. The aesthetic products of insanity as seen in the works of such people as William Blake, Vincent van Gogh, Jean Cocteau, and William Burroughs are frequently overlooked as being essential components of their creators' madness; such madness stigmatized and treated with drugs and confinement; stigmatization and status degradation.

Madness, The Work Ethic, and Self Actualization

The work ethic, which may be seen to inhibit self actualization in the form of peak experiences in the aesthetic modes of life, is not only all-pervasive but so powerful as to be mystified whereby self actualization is felt possible in an oppressive, ritualized environment. Where rules become ends in themselves; where there is a premium on thinking in narrow, rigid categories of thought; where personalities are molded into "methodical, prudent, disciplined"[8] entities; where work is a matter of life and death in a bureaucratic society, self actualization, or the more current term "wellness," is seen to be possible. Our socially constructed mystifications become reified and, lo and behold, work does in fact become a central life interest and source of self fulfillment for many people. To the degree that self actualization is desirable, and that bureaucratic necessities not only inhibit the attainment of such a goal, but mystify the experience to allow people to use work as the vehicle for its attainment, all work organizations share complicity. Some are more deceptive than others, by allowing "management by objectives" and "decentralization of decision making," (called Theory Y in the literature on organizations[9] but nevertheless have centralized policy making and have the recourse to suspension or curtailment of one's livelihood. It is this realization of one's economic and personal vulnerability that may yield the stigmatized madness of paranoia or the accepted madness of bureaucratic authoritarianism. The "methodical, prudent, disciplined" who need an inordinate amount of structure in their lives (and, apparently, in other people's lives) not only experience this self actualization at work, but are usually powerful and influential enough to expect work to be such a major source of fulfillment for other people as well. As they have the power (usually institutional power) to define sources of fulfillment for others, they thereby also have the power to define reality and appropriate behavior for other people as well, based upon their own constructions of this world. When their institutional power limits the personal autonomy necessary to cultivate the aesthetic mode of one's life, "sanity" not only becomes a political definition, but a vehicle for the "treatment" of a politically vulnerable group by representatives of a politically powerful group. In this scenario, "mental health" and "madness" are by no means necessarily contradictory.

Of course, the aesthetic mode of one's life is not only confined to artistic and poetic images. All people have the potential for active imaginations and fantasy lives. It is in the realm of the imagination that physical and spiritual ecstasy is possible. As has most frequently been pointed out by Transactional Analysts, "strokes", or signs of one's recognition, are essential to life, and in the absence of positive strokes, negative stroking (such as feeling guilt or being kicked) is better than no stroking at all.[10] As we grow older, we might be able to stroke ourselves with more effectiveness, particularly when most of our waking hours is spent working and living in relatively impersonal bureaucratic organizations, where such positive (or frequently even negative) stroking is at a premium.

Through an active imagination, self stroking is not only useful but enjoyable; it need not substitute for stroking by others (although it frequently has to) but may add a much needed dimension to one's happiness. As we can receive strokes through an active imagination, we may be seen to achieve states of self actualization or ecstasy in the same way. As the social world is constructed out of our imagination, and as many of its evils are constructed out of our imagination, so too are its delights. The nature of these delights and their intensity are not only products of our imagination, but need not necessarily be projected into or within other people's social worlds in order to be enjoyed and cherished (though they must if one is to avoid the label of "insanity"). To the degree that we have institutions in our society that legitimate ecstasy and exist solely or even primarily for that purpose, it is to that degree that an active imagination becomes crucial to prevent an existential withering away of people for whom ecstasy is not a luxury but a necessity of life not obtainable in oppressive institutions. It is a tragic irony that the degree to which an active imagination becomes necessary, it is to that degree that it is suppressed by rigid parenting and other rigid production-oriented institutions. The tragic irony becomes brutal when we realize that it is the functionaries of these oppressive institutions, frequently "loved ones" or family members, who define unacceptable products of the imagination as symptoms of illness and insist upon the treatment of the "illness" and the "confinement" of the one possessed.

Madness and Ecstasy

Self stroking can provide ecstasy and ecstasy certainly provides strokes. I am not suggesting that madness is always ecstasy. I am suggesting that it can be ecstasy; it can be a rational response to the oppressiveness of ritualized, non-stroking institutions in which both products and people are consumed. It seems ironic and ludicrous that the agents of these institutions are the ones who define needs for ecstasy, define madness, define its treatment, and politically impose their definitions of reality upon others, as psychiatrists and psychologists do by appearing as "expert witnesses" based upon questionable ideologies.

If bureaucracy is to survive at the expense of the cultivation of the aesthetic mode, people must be motivated to participate in this enterprise. The fear of deprivation of essential goods and services is the most basic of motivators. To the degree that one keenly realizes that it is in only products of the imagination that ecstasy may be achieved, those for whom ecstasy is a basic necessity or component of life will so cultivate the suitable imagery. Moreover, to the degree that one keenly realizes that he or she is extremely vulnerable to the vagaries of political and economic contingencies in a society, we may expect a greater likelihood of madness. This madness may occur either through conformity to the dictates of the bureaucratic mode or through the labeling by its staunch representatives of others who seek solace from the madness by going mad in a way the representatives neither understand nor condone. This latter type of madness is neither understood nor condoned because it is dysfunctional in a production-oriented society. The staunch representatives of the bureaucratic mode define and treat such madness as a withdrawal or escape. We may see forms of madness as a voluntary or an involuntary seeking for truth, and as a cultivation of the deepest recesses of the interior life.

One of the greatest threats to the bureaucratic mode is the institutionalization of ecstasy. Witness our draconian drug laws, and "war on drugs." Liberation of consciousness and the reification of images from the unconscious can be ecstatic. If they are painful, ecstasy may sometimes emerge through insightful nurturance of the seeker. To "treat" all such states as "illness," the society's representatives discount the potential for ecstasy and insight, degrade and stigmatize the one possessed, and are thus enabled to perpetuate the system in which they are so handsomely rewarded. For example, what would one do with an Isaiah or an Ezekiel and other prophets who saw aspects of God and reported His words to people who reviled both God and the "mad" prophets? For the mad seeker who does not accept the imposed images of the bureaucrat's madness, the mirror has more or less successfully, even if only temporarily, been turned to the wall."

NOTES

Revised version of a paper read at the annual meetings of the Pacific
Sociological Association, March, 1976.   A variation of this chapter also
appeared in my book, Essays on Deviance and Marginality, Lanham, Maryland:
University Press of America, 1979.

1. Kai T. Erikson, Wayward Puritans: A study in the Sociology of Deviance,
    New York: John Wiley and Sons., Inc., 1966, pp. 3-23.

2. Alfred Schutz, "Common Sense and Scientific Interpretation of Human
    Action," in M. Natanson, ed., Philosophy of the Social Sciences: A Reader,
    New York: Random House, 1963, pp. 302-46.

3. R. D. Laing, The Politics of Experience, New York: Ballantine Books,
    1968, p. 28.

4. Howard S. Becker, Outsiders: Studies in the Sociology of Deviance, New
    York: The Free Press, 1963, pp. 8-14.

5. William A. Rushing, "Two Patterns in the Relationship between Social
    Class and Mental Hospitalization," in W. Rushing, ed., Deviant Behavior
    and Social Process, Chicago: Rand McNally, 1975, pp. 395-402.

6. Jut Meininger, Success Through Transactional Analysis, New York: New
    American Library, 1973, pp. 25-33.

7. Jean Paul Sartre, Saint Genet: Actor and Martyr, New American Library,
    1971, p.9.

8. Robert Merton, "Bureaucratic Structure and Personality," in R. Merton, ed.,
    Social Theory and Social Structure, New York: The Free Press, 1968, pp.
    249-260.

9. See, for example, George Berkeley, The Administrative Revolution: Notes
    on the Passing of Organization Man, Englewood Cliffs, N.J.: Prentice
    Hall, Inc., 1971.

10. Jut Meininger, op.cit., p. 32.

11. The "Madness" to which I refer is one with which the bearer is content. Clearly, suffering people, involuntarily trapped by defects in their brain chemistry, are not dealt with in this context.

Chapter Five

Drug Use: The Institutionalization of Anesthesia and Ecstasy*

The discipline of Sociology was founded in a spirit of reform. Teachers and preachers signaled its coming as a way to ameliorate what they perceived to be the ills plaguing their society. Over the past decades much analysis has been done of many perceived social problems; in recent years that analysis has been increasingly more sophisticated, both quantitatively and qualitatively. Yet, we have forgotten the "promise." We were founded in the spirit of reform but have knowingly and unknowingly wound up as supposedly dispassionate handmaidens of the status quo. It seems that we will increasingly have to become more politically aggressive if we are to be true not only to our promise but true to the spirit of our analyses as well. The so-called drug problem in America is one example of this mandate.

There do not seem to be any institutions in our society where one may achieve ecstasy. Perhaps certain religious experiences yield such peak experiences; for most people, ecstasy-producing or ecstasy-inspiring institutions do not exist. Therefore, various forms of so-called deviant adaptations arise to fill the gap. The better one's socioeconomic status the more we may expect that he/she will experiment with drugs, be they legal or illegal. This correlation has certainly been established for marijuana use.[1] Perhaps this can be explained by relying on Maslow's notion of need hierarchy, where needs for self actualization may be expected to become more salient when one's physiological, safety, affiliative, and esteem needs are met.[2] Therefore, according to this logic, the more prosperous we become, the more we may strive for peak experiences. The poorer we are, drug use may be seen as an anesthetic for the pain of worthlessness that we have been taught to introject. Whereas both legal and illegal drugs are frequently used to reach these peak states in the best of times, they may also be used to aid in coping with life's problems in times of personal or economic depression. Indeed, drug use may be seen to serve as an anesthetic for the pains of living; the distinction between licit and illicit drugs has less to do with their pharmacological properties and toxicity than with the political prohibition against pleasure in a competitive, work-oriented society. For example, alcohol contributes to far more morbidity and mortality than does cocaine. Therefore, whether as an escape mechanism or as an ecstasy-producing mechanism, certain legal and illegal drugs do fill needs of people both in the best and in the worst of times.

I would like to briefly discuss the ecstasy that fills these needs for people. By the nature of my inquiry, my research has been unsystematic. Over the past several years, I have talked with users of a variety of drugs from legally prescribed tranquilizers to illegal marijuana, psychedelics, and opiates. Here, my concern has been with the nature of the "drug ecstasy" and the ecstasy-producing characteristics of various drugs. The drugs that I am concerned with here are opium, cocaine, and LSD.

Opium is typically smoked in a pipe, in which the tar-like material is placed. As with marijuana, the smoker holds the smoke deep in his/her lungs and slowly releases it. Opium creates an environment. The effects seem not to be related to the working of one's mind or perceptions as much as to an actual change in the environment of the person. The room, pictures on the walls, other people, seem surrounded by an aura or glow. It is quiet and peaceful. As with narcotics, one may realize she/he has problems, but has better things to do than dwell on them. It is easier to laugh than cry, but neither are worth the effort. Complex solutions are bothersome and unnecessary. The environment is peaceful and by looking at it, you are peaceful.

As opposed to opium, the ecstasy of cocaine is seemingly internal. Typically "snorted," it is also diluted and mainlined into the bloodstream via syringe. There is a mystique surrounding the cocaine high that is further abetted by its great cost (the current typical price being $100 or more a gram). Cocaine gives you confidence and security and a feeling of a quiet strength that leads to peace. The mundane is bothersome, as with narcotics; the mind is open to better enjoy the peace and pleasure of the "now." One doesn't want this feeling to end.

Acid is a psychedelic in that it allows one to see different levels of reality. The possibilities of everyday life are explored in an atmosphere of exaltation and joy. It is typically a very small tab that is swallowed with liquid. If words do not do justice to the opium or cocaine ecstasy, they actually defame the acid ecstasy. On acid, everything pulsates with energy. Colors change and glisten, leaves shine, and the mind projects images via its own film. The realization that all life is energy is coupled with the belief that all life is holy; the specifics of life are unimportant, but life goes on through eternity no matter what one does. Acid is a teacher, as opposed to cocaine and opium which produce pleasure (only pleasure). Poetry becomes crystal clear; television images become laughable in their perceived insidiousness. Categories of thought once held to be necessary are no longer so regarded; life situations are brought into a different perspective. As one person told me after his first acid experience, "I realized how lousy my life was and how I hated my job. I also realized that I brushed my teeth after every meal. Here I was talking such good care of my teeth, all the while I was losing my mind in a job I hated."

Despite the many criticisms of drug use (curiously and politically referred to as "drug abuse"), there are no institutions in our society that provide similar peak experiences or feelings of self actualization for most people in our society. Since frustrated desires for self-actualization experiences can be seen to lead to aggression and violence,[3] it is within the purview of social scientists to not only point out this fact, but provide suggested alternatives. At a time when violence has become institutionalized in our society, drug use may be seen to be socially beneficial. Indeed, as long as free space is continually constricted[4] so that there are no perceived frontiers for people to explore in social or ecological space; as long as the burgeoning middle class has increasing self-actualization needs; as long as the pain of life for many demands respite not only in the absence of pain but in the house of pleasure, drug use may be a viable method of obtaining this needed ecstasy in a simple, quick way.

It is probably incontestable that drugs such as opium and cocaine provide what comes closest to being the ultimate high possible; psychedelics, such as acid, a revered, ever-ready teacher. If our mission as social scientists is to not only analyze institutions and problems of society but to utilize our knowledge to help people, it seems appropriate that we suggest alternative ways of living and knowing based upon that knowledge. This may well be the ultimate thrust of the study of social problems in the future.

For example, if the data support such a contention, and I feel they do, drug-taking pavilions may be set up where people desirous of achieving ecstasy may come together and experience that joy; then subsequently go about their other routines. Alternative ways of living and knowing should be explored by social and behavioral scientists, their implications openly discussed, and conclusions and contentions posited in a politically aggressive and sophisticated way. Ecstasy is not a luxury but a necessity for many people; the more basic needs of food, clothing, shelter and association are met, the more we may expect increasing numbers of people to seek peak experiences; should be explored by social scientists who should not feel compelled to blindly accept the legal definitions of reality. Social scientists studying "social problems" will increasingly become sensitive to alternative ways to help people become fulfilled as human beings, and present and lobby for those alternatives we as an association can support, and that support will be contingent upon the data of research and discussion, and not upon dictates of the legal definitions of reality.

NOTES

*A variation of this chapter appeared in my book, Essays on Deviance and Marginality, Lanham, Maryland: University Press of America, 1979.

1. Erich Goode, Drugs in American Society, New York: Alfred A. Knopf, Inc., 1972, pp. 36-37.

2. Abraham H. Maslow, Motivation and Personality, New York: Harper and Brothers, 1954, p. 72. The relationship between self actualization and peak experiences is discussed by A.H. Maslow in his paper, "Peak Experiences as Acute Identity Experiences," American Journal of Psychoanalysis, 21, 1961, pp. 254-260.

3. John Dollard, et.al., Frustration and Aggression. New Haven: Yale University Press, 1939.

4. Stanford Lyman and Marvin Scott, "Territorality: A Neglected Sociological Dimension," in S. Lyman and M. Scott, A Sociology of the Absurd, New York: Appleton-Century-Crofts, 1970, pp. 89-109.

Chapter Six

A Proposal for Administrative Turnover*

In a time when college and university enrollments are shifting due to market, student interest, and demographic shifts, increasing attention has been paid to the need for a qualified, flexible faculty. One answer to this problem has been to structurally build in turnover into the university among the faculty ranks. In this way, it is felt that flexibility can be assured by preventing any one unit from tenuring 100% of its faculty, and quality can be obtained given the relative plethora of qualified applicants for teaching positions, due to the relatively poor job market in college teaching.

On the other hand, these requisites are imposed by administrators who are not only relatively well entrenched in their positions, but are frequently paid far higher than faculty at the same step; there are administrators who neither possess the terminal degree nor have a department of record who similarly benefit from such a great pay differential. Moreover, except under relatively rare circumstances, administrators do not seem desirous of "returning to the classroom," if they are able to do so. This occurrence is understandable, particularly given the differentials of power (or discretion and influence), prestige, and wealth of administrators vis a' vis most faculty.

As a department chairman and colleague, I am very much concerned with the ever-increasing need for flexibility and quality in the relatively austere market in which we find ourselves. However, this quality and flexibility must not only be imposed upon faculty, but upon administrators as well. It is unfortunate that a dichotomy between the two must be made. However, both the Sociology of Knowledge (which tells us that one's ideas and ideologies are based upon his or her position in the social structure), and the concept of "role-determined personality" (which emphasizes the sociological truism that one's role or roles have a pervasive effect upon his or her attitudes and view of the world) make it virtually impossible to ignore this dichotomy. Moreover, this dichotomy may be observed by differences in salary and concomitant styles of life of both faculty and administrators.

Although discussion implicitly and explicitly regarding faculty turnover is relatively extensive, with emphasis placed upon "accountability," Student Evaluation of Faculty, as well as the aforementioned emphasis upon "flexibility," similar concerns regarding administrative turnover in higher education do not seem as apparent. Moreover, this academic "double-standard" seems mirrored by the seemingly low degree of awareness and/or concern on the part of a great many faculty--particularly the older and tenured among us--for whom the dicta regarding flexibility and turnover and, indeed, "quality," are not as easily enforced (to put it mildly).

Indeed, it may be expected given this degree of awareness and double standard that administrative review committees would be far more loathe to "fire" or in some other way publicly censure an administrator than would a personnel committee or chairman be loathe to deny tenure (or even promotion) to a colleague.

Of course, this paper in no way implies "evil" or incompetence on the part of the general population of administrators. This is far from the case. My own experience has shown most of them to be sincere, dedicated people trying to do the best job they know how under increasingly difficult circumstances. The intent of this paper is to address the need for flexibility in the administrative ranks to enhance colleagueship between faculty and administrators on the one hand, and to continually build a reservoir of concerned and aware faculty on the other, and institutionally build in consistency in salary among as many faculty as possible.

The implementation of these goals, of course, is not an easy task, and no one set of recommendations at this juncture need or should be definitive. However, I am making the following recommendations as "food for thought":

1. There must be mandatory turnover of all administrators, with the exception of the President.
2. The implementation of #1 insures that no department chair, dean, associate vice president, or any other associated administrator may serve in that capacity for more than a specified period.
3. Continuity of administrators and familiarity with the office as well as flexibility will be served if no administrator may serve more than five consecutive years in an administrative capacity. One feasible way of implementing this item is to have a probationary period of two years and a definite term for up to three more upon successful completion of that probationary term as judged by an Executive Review and Selection Committee and the President.
4. Should an administrator seek another administrative post within the University, it may only be in an amount not to exceed the five year period under which he or she now works.

5. If an administrator wishes to seek another administrative post within the university after he has served the five years as an administrator, he or she must serve at least five consecutive years teaching full-time at this or another university, before being considered for such a position.

6. No administrator may receive more salary than a faculty member on a 12-month appointment at the equivalent rank and step; no faculty member may be given an accelerated promotion for assuming an administrative post. The criteria for accelerated promotion must be the same for teacher and administrative faculty.

The implementation of these recommendations may be expected to do the following:

1. Insure continuity of administration and familiarity with the particular role.

2. Help prevent a tendency toward oligarchy, despite the best of intentions and motives of the people involved.

3. Keep all colleagues in touch with the realities of teaching and its attendant rewards and problems.

4. Encourage the building up of a reservoir of concerned, knowledgeable faculty regarding the many roles of the university outside the classroom.

5. Help increase collegiality and make more apparent the notion of the university as a true "community of scholars."

6. Help erase the discretionary and salary discrepancies now apparent and seemingly inimical to colleagueship.

I truly believe that implementation of these recommendations, or recommendations like them, will bring a breath of fresh air to a university and allow all of us to pursue scholarship and administration as colleagues in the truest sense of the word.

*Written fall 1974 and appeared in the University Journal, California State University, Chico.

Chapter Seven

Annual Faculty Senate Report to the General Faculty—California State University, Chico

Jerry Maneker, Chair - May 12, 1982

I would like to take this opportunity to share with you some of my perceptions of the University, particularly as we enter this era of collective bargaining. These words are written with some feeling and hope that you do not misunderstand my intentions given the dual role I have occupied: President of a faculty union chapter and Chair of the Faculty Senate. Since the representation of the faculty is paramount to both these offices, and that in both these offices the incumbents serve at the pleasure of the faculty, certain qualms may be groundless. Yet, what remain I hasten to address by assuring you that my passionate embrace of collective bargaining is a recognition of our profound vulnerability. What helped bring collective bargaining about was a lack of true shared governance, and the lack of a vigorous Faculty Senate, and the ensuing consequences of what can only be described as an appalling callousness regarding our financial remuneration and the quality of education in our system.

So my comments come from a person for whom collective bargaining was a last resort, a last gasp act of desperation to salvage what professional pride, educational quality, salutary working conditions, and remuneration is possible in a society that largely turns its back on its teachers, scholars, and artists. The University is the last haven for us "misfits," and we must, therefore, take an active part in nurturing it. There is nowhere else to go, and so to the degree that we are threatened with cutbacks of money, resources, pride, respect, we grasp at the straws that become available. There are two such straws that present themselves--collective bargaining and university governance. I have done my best to address the former in a variety of contexts, so I would like to take this opportunity to briefly address this other, this second, perhaps, final straw. And I want to preface my remarks by affirming my fondness for many of the people of the Senate and for many of the people with whom I have dealt as its Chair. I sincerely hope that my remarks will not offend the people who have given a great deal of themselves in serving the university by participation on the Senate. In no way do I intend to demean their efforts or accomplishments.

In my opinion, we have suffered unnecessary polarization of faculty and administration in our university within the past couple of years. The concept of "shared governance" has been seriously compromised. In some very important matters, either consultation with the Senate has not occurred, or has occurred after the fact. In these matters administrative decisions have either reflected apparent disdain or disregard of faculty insight or involvement. Moreover, one has no reason to believe that such occurrences will not continue over the long run, perhaps using the existence of collective bargaining as justification. It would be easy to solely blame the administration for these occurrences. Yet the faculty, too, are to blame as we have enabled these occurrences to happen in the first place through our complacency, weakness, avarice, or selfishness.

We have over the past several years suffered a rather weak Faculty Senate. We have recruited people to its ranks some of whom sought to use it to their own advantage. Some joined so they could add a line on their Personal Data Sheet to help facilitate tenure or promotion. Some others joined so they could be knighted into administration; who comport themselves in a manner consistent with the values of an institution that views administration as a step up from faculty status, as a means of upward mobility. Rather than join the Faculty Senate to serve the highest ideals of the intellectual and academic life, as well as to serve the varied interests of one's colleagues, these people wittingly or unwittingly sold out--sold out the trust placed in them by their colleagues, as well as the vision of a civilized, life-enhancing institution in which to work. Yet, faculty have expected and perhaps deserved no more than this. For if many of us have, it has not been observable to me. Non-Senators too partake in this culpability to the degree they actively or passively partake in a studied enmity or indifference to matters of university governance. And many faculty seem to view with aplomb the obsequious careerists who seem to come from nowhere, adopt whatever image is salable, and thereby assume the mantle of academic leaders. Please seriously search for what substance there is behind these carefully presented images. Image is no substitute for substance.

One of the rules I try to live by is "If you don't use it, you lose it." This rule can certainly be applied to university governance. Yet for faculty to be actively involved in university governance we must overcome what I perceive to be a deeply entrenched timidity among our faculty. Perhaps it's due to our idealism and desire to live more of the interior life than economic and political reality allow. We prefer to think the best of people, and we hate unpleasantness. Yet such burning issues as layoffs at one or more of our sister institutions scarcely raises an eyebrow. We certainly do not actively express our concerns and we do not seem to empathize sufficiently to realize that we are not immune to such occurrences. We have become unwitting martinets, accessories, and hostages to fortune of activities that normalize faculty vulnerability to what has been euphemistically called "retrenchment." Many of these results are consequences of the belief held by many that teachers should teach and do research, and that administration should be left up to the administrators. If we persist in this belief, we will reap a whirlwind far more disastrous than that from which we have already suffered. Active involvement in university governance and eternal vigilance are absolutely essential.

What we need is a strong Faculty Senate and a strong faculty. We need a faculty composed of people who feel confident in their professional abilities, who feel there is no greater calling than the work they do. We need more faculty who do not abdicate responsibility for any academic or professional matters to do with a university to functionaries who should exist to make life easier for them, and not ride roughshod overly deeply held sensibilities of the most sensitive and dedicated of our number.

We are perhaps the only profession that lacks an esprit de corps, a consciousness of kind, and for this lapse we have paid and will continue to pay dearly in morale, salary, perquisites, and hegemony over our working conditions. And the cost goes deeper yet. It affects our relations with each other, our self-image, and our spiritual quest for meaning in the quality of our work. The stakes are far greater than the suffering of such insults as administrative caprice. They go deep into the fabric of the nature of our university; our self image as professionals or civil servants; our relations with students as either clients to be served or as constituents to be pleased, or as adversaries to be co-opted; our relations with each other as befit scholars pursuing a calling or civil servants treating each others as commodities. I urge you to please take our Senate seriously, and not for granted. Many hard-won gains of the past can easily be eroded through our indolence. Support your Senators, read the minutes of our Senate meetings, make your wishes and needs known to your representatives, and actively involve yourselves in the governance of our university. A weak Senate is worse than no Senate at all. A weak Senate may be used as a tool for petty and not so petty intrigues by either the Administration, the Bargaining Agent, or by both of these groups. We must do our very best to have as strong a Senate as possible. Insist on a strong Senate. Expect and demand the very best we have to offer.

In closing I want to take this opportunity to express my gratitude to my constituents in the School of Behavioral and Social Sciences who elected me to represent them for the past two years, as well s to many of my fellow Senators, particularly those on the Faculty Policies Committee, with whom I thoroughly enjoyed working. I also want to express my profound appreciation to Sylvia Brown, who runs the Senate office with competence and efficiency that does us all great service, and who made this intruder into her midst feel welcome and grateful for that.

Chapter Eight

Some Sociological Aspects of Racism on College Campuses*

Racism is as likely to exist and flourish in institutions of higher education as in any other institution in society. It would be a mistake to think that the college campus differs significantly on various organizational dimensions from other institutions in society. The college campus is a bureaucracy, a people-processing institution in society of which it is a part and whose interests it serves. Rather than being "proactive," it is almost always "reactive," taking its cues from the society and its constituents. Therefore, college campuses are usually quite conservative, primarily populated with civil servants whose careers are largely circumscribed by the bureaucracy in which they work; the articulation of whose expertise is made possible by that bureaucracy. As was pointed out many years ago by Robert Merton, bureaucracy coerces its participants to be "methodical, prudent, disciplined." (Robert Merton, "Bureaucratic Structure and Personality," in his book <u>Social Theory and Social Structure</u>.) Such people are not likely to take make waves or take stands without using the organization within which they work as a compass point to determine their responses to controversial, and even many-non-controversial, issues.

As a reactive institution, the university campus reflects the larger society of which it is a part. This larger society, particularly over the past several years, has allowed greed, hedonism, materialism, and self-absorption to run rampant and become validated as components of a lifestyle increasingly viewed as viable. Social scientists have long known that such values and the class conflicts they both foster and represent conduce toward racism. As Eliot Aronson points out. "...the dominant group might attempt to exploit or derogate a minority group in order to gain some material advantage. Prejudiced attitudes tend to increase when times are tense and there is conflict over mutually exclusive goals. This is true whether the goals are economic, political, or ideological.... Discrimination, prejudice, and negative stereotyping increase sharply as competition for scarce jobs increases....data indicate that competition and conflict breed prejudice."

(Eliot Aronson, The Social Animal, pp. 245-247.) We also have increasing violence in the streets and the thrust of dealing with the symptom of social malaise and dislocation is to build more prisons, have greater police presence in inner cities to, in effect, further colonize the poor and minorities who live there, and have convenient, simplistic slogans to complex problems such as "just say no." Such approaches bespeak our lack of interest in reforming the institutions that do not adequately address and meet human and social needs. We do not bother to ask why young people are so disaffected that they take inordinate risks to their health and well- being, to shoot drugs, prey upon others for what gratification is available to them, and frequently become old men and women by the time they are fifteen years of age. We respond to their plight by still believing and promulgating the Horatio Alger myth.

We cannot ignore the statistics. In the richest country in the world, we have inordinate homelessness, and inadequate housing affecting perhaps ten million of our citizens, according to Mitch Snyder (C-SPAN, 8-22-89), the well-known advocate for the homeless. We see the economic dislocation between men and women full time workers where in 1986 the median income for men was $25,894 and for women was $16,834. (Leonard Beeghley, The Structure of Social Stratification in the United States, 1987, p. 239.) Comparing white and black males with at least four years of college we again see the economic dislocation. In 1987, the median income for white males with at least four years of college was $32,048 and for black males in this category, $21,988. White and black women in this category was $23,749 and $21,140 respectively. (U.S. Department of Commerce, Bureau of the Census, "Money Income of Households, Families and Persons in the Unites States:1987.) It has been found that there is discrimination against Mexican American college graduate by private firms which amounts to twelve percent of Anglo earnings. (Raymond and Sesnowitz, "Labor Market Discrimination Against Mexican American College Graduates," Southern Economics Journal, April 1983, pp. 1122-1136.) Moreover, in 1984 the Census Bureau reported that "the net worth of the typical white American household...was 12 times as great as the figure for the typical black household and eight times as great as the typical net worth of Latinos." Nearly one-third of all black households and one-quarter of Latinos had no net assets or were in debt. Fewer than one in ten whites had no assets at all." (L.A. Times, July 19, 1986, p. 1, col. 3.)

So if our society embodies values where it appears that the worst crime you can commit is to be poor, discriminates against minorities for economic, political, ideological, and psychological gains, oversees increasing disparities of wealth when comparing the dominant and minority elements in our population, even among college graduates, what can educational institutions do? If educational institutions are reactive, insular and conservative, how may they be used to address racism? The following points may help.

1. We must recognize that "intelligence" and "education" are not synonymous. I have known very intelligent high school dropouts, and some PhD's who are very limited human beings. It seems to be that intelligence does more to enhance one's education than one's education does to enhance his or her intelligence. Some highly educated people are racists. For example, many of the people of Hitler's staff had university degrees. Education confers no immunity to racist inclinations or actions.

2. Since the 1930s, educational philosophy has become pragmatic. Rather than asking "Is this right or wrong?" we ask "Does this work?" It seems that universities have increasingly promulgated a vocational emphasis, and emphasis upon one's career, and downplayed or ignored ethics and moral sensibilities, without which one can be educated, but not intelligent. Intelligence presupposes a sense of right and wrong, a sense of honor and integrity, justice and humility that must be integrated into the courses we teach. We must by word and example show forth "agape" love. Unlike 'Eros' which is self-oriented or "phileo" which is love based upon reciprocity of favors, agape requires an act of will whereby we put another person's feelings and interests ahead of our own, regardless of our feelings toward that person. The cultivation of agape is an essential step in inculcating the moral sensibilities necessary to make one truly intelligent, as opposed to being a formally educated bibliophile. It is lack of moral sensibilities that can easily lead to hate. To be effective, education must be morally sensible. Such belief systems in the social sciences and education as "situation ethics" and "moral relativism" seem to have compromised moral integrity and social ethics. The fact is ethics do transcend situations; there is absolute truth whether we care to face it or not. No one doubts this contention when we add a column of figures, but when such absolute truth offends our values or puts us at a perceived disadvantage, we take umbrage and retreat to moral relativism.

3. Academic work is frequently seen as only one part of the college experience, perhaps somewhat less important than the acquisition of social skills and the development of a "well-rounded person." Frequently, the outcome of such a stance is that values of indolence and manipulation of others are learned and viewed as more useful than critical thinking concerning the world we live in and our role in that world. Academic work, if done correctly, forces the student to confront the moral code he/she serves. For each of us does serve one. To emphasize the social aspects of the college experience, and thereby place a premium on becoming "other directed," in my opinion, conduces to merely reflecting the values of our larger society, some of which result in racism, and other brutalities; inhibits the courage it takes to recognize and live up to the moral imperatives that would minimize racism and its effects. Therefore, we must demand intellectual rigor coupled with moral sensibility in our classes. We must encourage the students to express their values regarding individual and group diversity and other salient issues so that these values can be explored, clarified, and made answerable to data that have been obtained.

4. Since education is not the answer to racism, we must encourage our students to use education, and not let it use them. Particularly in the humanities and social sciences, we must encourage them to read and integrate, through questions and discussion, such trenchant writers and thinkers in this areas as James Baldwin, Franz Fanon, Dee Brown, Vine DeLoria, Malcolm X, Piri Thomas, Claude Brown, so that students may learn from them and introject their teachings and experiences into their own lives.

5. A liberal education must enjoin the student to not allow other people to define his or her reality. We must explicitly ask them the questions "What are you learning, and from whom are you learning? Everyone learns. Is what you are learning supported by evidence? Is it useful? Is it edifying? Is it morally sensible, that is, does it make moral sense? Does it recognize that we are literally all brothers and sisters?" We do come from the same original parents, you know. The student must be told that when learning, he or she must insist that all contentions made be supported by data. It doesn't matter how may titles a person has after his or her name, the student must insist that data be presented to support the values implied or expressed. Students must be encouraged to be tough minded; be disciplined learners (disciples) in that they are very much involved in what they learn, how they learn, and by whom they learn.

6. We must tell them that they must be more "inner directed." A human being must not let his or her intellectual, emotional, and spiritual intactness as a person be unduly influenced by other people, even if they are
   well-intentioned. The student should be told that one must keep one's goal(s) firmly in mind and cultivate his or her talents and not to expect others to necessarily recognize or appreciate those talents or necessarily affirm him or her as a person.

7. Unfortunately, most people only respond to an issue when their ox is the one being gored. For many, racism, is not an issue unless they are the recipient of the hostility, the gratuitous brutality, the gentlemen's agreement, the social and personal discounting attendant upon racist values. All students, particularly minority students, must be told to not introject feelings of unworthiness. Nor is it healthy to externalize rage. They must be given permission to stand their ground and expose racism wherever it occurs in the situation in which one finds him/herself, whether or not one is the recipient of the racism. In universities, we must all confront racism in all of its aspects--from the seemingly "harmless" ethnic or sexist joke to its more egregious manifestations; write letters to the responsible parties both within and outside the given institution; write letters to the editor of the local and other major newspapers where deemed appropriate; utilize the courts where deemed necessary; discuss racism and other types of hate mongering as they apply to the course material in classes to sensitize others and ourselves as to their destructiveness and violation of the goals the intellectual life should afford and encourage.